WORLD MYTHOLOGY

VENUS

B. A. Hoena

Consultant:

Dr. Laurel Bowman
Department of Greek and Roman Studies
University of Victoria, British Columbia

Capstone
press

Mankato, Minnesota

Capstone Press
151 Good Counsel Drive, P.O. Box 669, Mankato, Minnesota 56002
http://www.capstonepress.com

Library of Congress Cataloging-in-Publication Data
Hoena, B. A.
  Venus / B. A. Hoena.
    p. cm.—(World mythology)
  Summary: Relates the exploits of Venus and her importance in Roman mythology,
including her connection to such figures as Aeneus and Adonis, and describes the role of
myths in the modern world.
  Includes bibliographical references and index.
  ISBN 0-7368-3457-5 (paperback) ISBN 0-7368-1612-7 (hardcover)
  1. Venus (Roman deity)—Juvenile literature. [1. Venus (Roman deity) 2. Mythology,
Roman.] I. Title. II. Series.
BL820.V5 H64 2003
292.2'114—dc21   2002008465

Editorial Credits
Karen Risch, product planning editor; Juliette Peters, designer and illustrator;
    Alta Schaffer, photo researcher

Photo Credits
Art Resource/Erich Lessing, 4, 10; Scala, 8, 12; Réunion des Musées Nationaux, 14, 18;
    Alinari, 16
Corbis/Araldo de Luca, cover; Geoffrey Clements, 20 (left)
PhotoDisc, Inc./StockTrek, 20 (right)

1 2 3 4 5 6 08 07 06 05 04 03

TABLE OF CONTENTS

This Roman statue of Venus was made around 330 B.C.
In art, Venus often is shown with her son Cupid (left).

VENUS

In Roman myths, Venus (VEE-nuhss) was the goddess of love and marriage. She also was the goddess of beauty. Myths say that Venus was more beautiful than any other goddess. Ancient Greeks called her Aphrodite (a-fruh-DYE-tee).

Venus was one of the 12 Olympians. Ancient Greeks and Romans believed these powerful gods ruled the world from Mount Olympus. This mountain is in central Greece. People thought Mount Olympus rose so high that it touched the heavens.

Ancient Greeks and Romans believed the gods controlled every part of their lives. People often prayed to the different gods for help. People prayed to Minerva (muh-NUR-vuh), the goddess of wisdom, for advice. They prayed to Neptune (NEP-toon), the god of the sea, for safe sea voyages. Venus was one of the most popular Olympians. People asked her to help them find love.

GREEK and ROMAN *Mythical Figures*

Greek Name: **APHRODITE**
Roman Name: **VENUS**
Goddess of love and beauty

Greek Name: **APOLLO**
Roman Name: **APOLLO**
God of youth and music

Greek Name: **ATHENA**
Roman Name: **MINERVA**
Goddess of wisdom

Greek Name: **ARES**
Roman Name: **MARS**
God of war

Greek Name: **CRONUS**
Roman Name: **SATURN**
Titan who ruled the heavens
before the Olympians

Greek Name: **EROS**
Roman Name: **CUPID**
Venus' son and god of love

Greek Name: **HEPHAESTUS**
Roman Name: **VULCAN**
Venus' husband and god of fire

Greek Name: **HERA**
Roman Name: **JUNO**
Zeus' wife and goddess of
marriage and childbirth

Greek Name: **POSEIDON**
Roman Name: **NEPTUNE**
Zeus' brother and god of the sea

Greek Name: **ZEUS**
Roman Name: **JUPITER**
Ruler of the Olympians

ABOUT MYTHOLOGY

The word myth comes from the Greek word *mythos*. It means tale or story. Mythology is a collection of stories.

Ancient Greeks and Romans did not know how to explain the world scientifically. They did not know why earthquakes and storms happened. Instead, people told myths to help them explain these events. Myths about Venus explained how and why people fell in love.

Ancient Greeks and Romans also used myths to explain the source of things. One example was the myth of Adonis (uh-DAH-nuhss). It explained the origin of roses.

Myths say that Adonis was the most handsome man in the world. Even the gods were amazed by his beauty. Venus loved Adonis. Her love for Adonis angered Mars, the god of war. He killed Adonis because he loved Venus.

Adonis' blood fell to the ground as Venus cried over his dead body. Roses grew where Adonis' blood touched the ground. Roses became one of Venus' symbols and represent love.

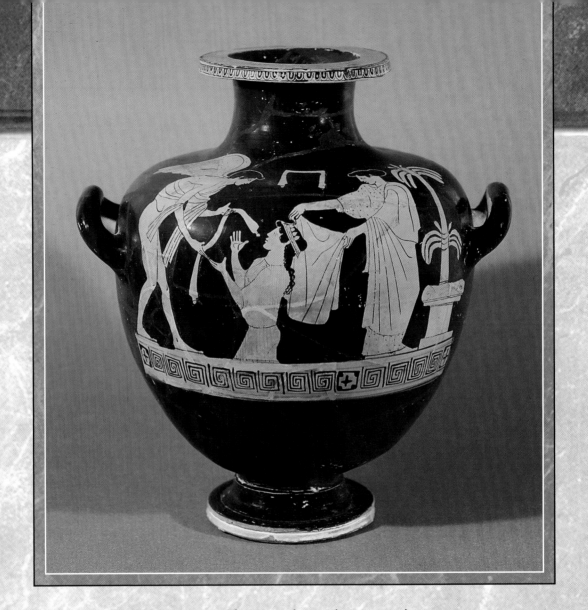

Artists often show scenes from myths in their art. This ancient vase shows a scene from Venus' (center) birth. The two standing figures are nymphs. They are offering clothes to Venus after she washed ashore.

THE BIRTH OF VENUS

Before the Olympians, Gaea (JEE-uh) ruled the earth. Uranus (YUR-uh-nuhss) ruled the heavens. Their children were powerful giants called Titans.

Uranus was jealous of his children's power. He was afraid they might grow stronger than he was. Uranus locked up the Titans to prevent them from overthrowing him as ruler of the heavens.

Uranus' actions saddened Gaea. She wanted her children to live freely on the earth. She decided to help her son Saturn (SAT-urn) overthrow his father.

One night, Saturn sneaked up on his father and cut him with a knife. A piece of Uranus' body then fell into the sea. The sea began to foam where it landed. Myths say that Venus grew from the foamy water. Venus' Greek name, Aphrodite, means "born of foam." She then washed up onto the shore fully grown.

Afterward, Saturn became ruler of the heavens. Many of the Olympians are his children.

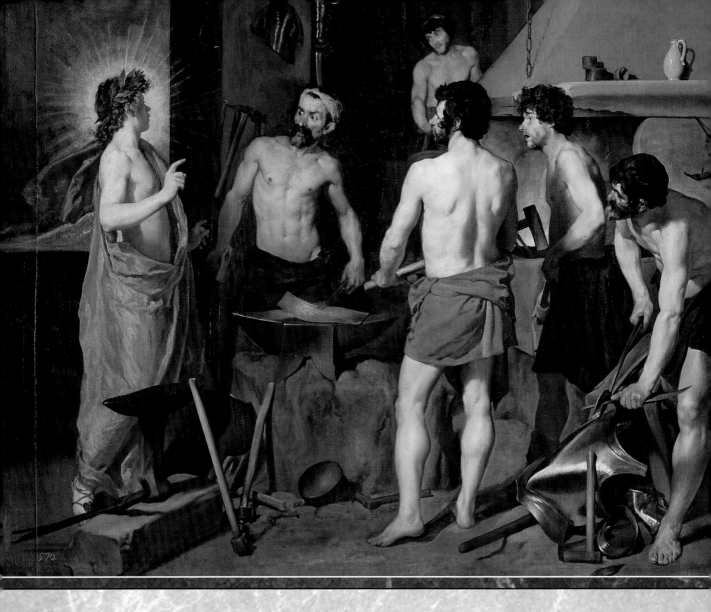

This painting shows Apollo (left) talking to Vulcan (center). Apollo was the god of youth and music. He is telling Vulcan that Venus has not been a loyal wife.

THE GODDESS OF LOVE

Saturn's son Jupiter (JOO-puh-tur) ruled the Olympians.
He saw how all the male gods fell in love with Venus' beauty.
He worried they would start arguing about her. To prevent
them from fighting, Jupiter made Venus marry his son
Vulcan (VUHL-kan). Vulcan was the god of fire.

Venus was not happy with her marriage. Myths say that
Vulcan was ugly compared to other gods. Venus was not a loyal
wife to him. She had children with other gods.

Cupid (KYOO-pid) was her son with Mars. Cupid was the
god of love. Artists often show him as a young boy with wings.
Cupid shot people with magical arrows. People struck by these
arrows fell in love.

Aeneas (i-NEE-uhss) was another son of Venus. He was
famous for leading the people of Troy to Italy. Aeneas led them
there after a Greek army attacked the city of Troy. This battle is
known as the Trojan War.

Giandomenico Tiepolo's painting *Farewell of Venus to Aeneas* shows the goddess of love saying goodbye to her son. Ancient Romans believed Aeneas founded their people after sailing to Italy.

ROMAN VERSUS GREEK MYTHS

The Romans captured Greece about 100 B.C. The Romans often adopted parts of culture from the countries they took over. Many stories in Roman mythology are copied from Greek myths.

The Romans and Greeks also used some of the same characters in their myths. But the Romans gave many of their gods different names. Aphrodite is the Greek name for Venus. Hephaestus (he-FESS-tuhss) is the Greek name for Venus' husband, Vulcan.

The Romans also changed the importance of some gods. The Greeks believed Aphrodite was the goddess of lawless passions. She had many lovers and was often disloyal to her husband. The Romans placed importance on home life. They thought of Venus as the goddess of love and marriage.

Ancient Romans even used a Greek myth to explain their origins. They believed the hero Aeneas sailed to Italy after the Trojan War. There, he founded the Roman people.

In this piece of art, Paris is on the left. To the far right are Minerva, Juno, and Venus. They are waiting for Paris to pick who is the most beautiful goddess.

THE TROJAN WAR

Myths say that an argument between Venus, Juno (JOO-noh), and Minerva led to the Trojan War. These goddesses argued about who was more beautiful. Jupiter told Paris to choose which goddess was the most beautiful. Paris was a prince of the city of Troy.

Each goddess promised Paris a special gift if he picked her. Paris chose Venus. She had promised to give him Helen as his wife. In myths, Helen was the most beautiful woman in the world.

Paris married Helen. But Helen was already married to a Greek prince. This prince became angry that Helen had been taken from him. He sent an army to Troy to get Helen back from Paris.

These events started the Trojan War. Many Greek and Trojan heroes fought in this 10-year battle. In *The Iliad*, the Greek poet Homer tells about the Trojan War's last year. His long poem tells how the Greeks defeated the people of Troy.

In myths, Mars (left, standing) and Venus (left, sitting) spent a great deal of time together. Their son Cupid stands in the center of the painting.

VENUS AND MARS

Venus loved Mars. He was very strong and handsome. Venus and Mars often spent time together.

One day, Vulcan found out that Venus and Mars were spending time together. He became very angry. He wanted to teach them a lesson.

Vulcan made a strong, magic net. He hung the net over Venus' bed. He then told Venus that he was leaving for several days.

Mars visited Venus as soon as he thought Vulcan had left. But Vulcan was only hiding. When he saw Mars and Venus together, he let the net drop on them. Mars and Venus were trapped beneath the net.

Vulcan told the other Olympians about Venus and Mars. The Olympians laughed at the two gods trapped in Vulcan's net. Venus and Mars became very embarrassed. They stayed away from each other for a long time afterward.

This painting by Noel Halle shows Hippomenes winning the
race against Atalanta. Atalanta is bending down to pick
up one of the gold apples that Venus gave Hippomenes.

HIPPOMENES AND ATALANTA

In myths, people often asked Venus to help them find love. Hippomenes (hi-PUH-mee-ness) prayed to her when he wanted to marry Atalanta (a-tuhl-AN-tuh). Atalanta did not want to marry. But her father hoped she would get married. To make him happy, Atalanta promised to marry the first man who beat her in a race. Atalanta ran very fast and never lost a race.

Venus gave Hippomenes three gold apples to help him. She told him how he could use these apples to marry Atalanta. Hippomenes then challenged Atalanta to a race.

Atalanta took an early lead in the race. Hippomenes then threw one of the apples in front of her. Atalanta thought the apple was beautiful and stopped to pick it up. Hippomenes raced past her, but she quickly caught up. Hippomenes threw another apple. Again, he raced past Atalanta as she stopped, but she caught up once more. Hippomenes then threw the last apple. When Atalanta stopped, Hippomenes ran past her and won the race. Afterward, they got married.

Venus' son Cupid (left) is a symbol of love. His image often is used on Valentine's Day cards. The planet Venus (below) was named after the Roman goddess of love.

MYTHOLOGY TODAY

Mythical names are common today. Early astronomers thought the second planet from the Sun looked beautiful. They named it Venus after the goddess of beauty. All the other planets are named after Roman gods such as Jupiter, Mars, and Neptune.

Artists often use figures from myths in their art. Artists create sculptures and paintings of Venus and other mythical characters. People have written songs about Venus. In stories and poems, authors compare beautiful women to Venus.

People use many of Venus' symbols. Valentine's Day decorations often show her son Cupid. People give loved ones roses on this day. Doves are another one of Venus' symbols. Roses and doves often are part of wedding decorations.

People no longer believe in Greek and Roman myths. They do not believe that gods on Mount Olympus control their lives. Today, people tell myths simply for each other's enjoyment.

Adriatic Sea

•Rome

ITALY

N
W • E
S

GREECE

•Troy

Aegean Sea

Thebes

ITHACA

Ionian Sea

Athens

Sparta

DELOS

SCALE
Miles
0   100   200

0   100   200
Kilometers

CRETE

Mediterranean Sea

KEY

• City

Oracle of Delphi

Mount Olympus

Region of Attica

WORDS TO KNOW

adopt (uh-DOPT)—to accept an idea or a way of doing things

ancient (AYN-shunt)—very old

culture (KUHL-chur)—a people's way of life, ideas, art, customs, and traditions

nymph (NIMF)—a female spirit or goddess found in a meadow, a forest, a mountain, or a stream

Olympian (oh-LIM-pee-uhn)—one of the 12 powerful gods who lived on Mount Olympus in Greece

origin (OR-uh-jin)—the cause or source of something

overthrow (oh-vur-THROH)—to defeat a leader and remove the person from power

Titan (TYE-ten)—one of the giants who ruled the world before the Olympians

Trojan (TROH-jin)—having to do with the city of Troy

READ MORE

Lively, Penelope. *In Search of a Homeland: The Story of The Aeneid.* New York: Delacorte Press, 2001.

Nardo, Don. *Roman Mythology.* History of the World. San Diego: Kidhaven Press, 2002.

USEFUL ADDRESSES

**National Junior Classical
    League**
Miami University
Oxford, OH 45056

Ontario Classical Association
2072 Madden Boulevard
Oakville, ON L6H 3L6
Canada

INTERNET SITES

Track down many sites about Venus.
Visit the FACT HOUND at *http://www.facthound.com*

IT IS EASY! IT IS FUN!

1) Go to *http://www.facthound.com*
2) Type in: 0736816127
3) Click on "FETCH IT" and FACT HOUND
   will find several links hand-picked by our editors.

Relax and let our pal FACT HOUND do the research for you!

INDEX